Watch Me Go!

MY SLED

Victor Blaine

PowerKiDS press™

New York

Published in 2015 by The Rosen Publishing Group, Inc.
29 East 21st Street, New York, NY 10010

First Edition

Editor: Sarah Machajewski
Book Design: Mickey Harmon

Photo Credits: Cover, pp. 1, 17 (inset), 22 Sergey Novikov/Shutterstock.com; p. 5 gorillaimages/Shutterstock.com; p. 6 Smailhodzic/Shutterstock.com; p. 9 (main) Gina Smith/Shutterstock.com; p. 9 (inset) MARGRIT HIRSCH/Shutterstock.com; p. 10 Nate Allred/Shutterstock.com; p. 13 Maria Pavlova/E+/Getty Images; p. 14 pavla/Shutterstock.com; p. 17 (main) Design Pics/Ron Nickel/Getty Images; p. 18 Dmitry Kalinovsky/Shutterstock.com; p. 21 Steve Mason/Photodisc/Getty Images.

Library of Congress Cataloging-in-Publication Data

Blaine, Victor.
My sled / by Victor Blaine.
p. cm. — (Watch me go!)
Includes index.
ISBN 978-1-4994-0257-5 (pbk.)
ISBN 978-1-4994-0242-1 (6-pack)
ISBN 978-1-4994-0249-0 (library binding)
1. Sledding — Juvenile literature. I. Title.
GV856.B53 2015
796.9—d23

Manufactured in the United States of America

CPSIA Compliance Information: Batch #CW15PK: For Further Information contact Rosen Publishing, New York, New York at 1-800-237-9932

CONTENTS

Have you ever been on a sled?

Sleds are fun to use in winter.
They move fast on snow
and ice.

Some sleds are made of wood.
Some sleds are made of plastic.

wooden sleds

plastic sled

One kind of sled is called a **toboggan**. Toboggans are long sleds.

Some sleds have **runners**.
The runners help a sled slide
on the snow.

Sleds without runners have a smooth bottom. This makes the sled move fast!

Some sleds carry just one person. Big sleds carry many people.

Sleds aren't just for people! Some dogs know how to pull sleds.

Horses pull sleds, too. These sleds are called sleighs.

Sledding is a fun way
to get around!

WORDS TO KNOW

runner   toboggan

INDEX

WEBSITES

Due to the changing nature of Internet links, PowerKids Press has developed an online list of websites related to the subject of this book. This site is updated regularly. Please use this link to access the list: www.powerkidslinks.com/wmg/sled